The Illustrated

Wrinklies' Wit & Wisdom

First published in 2005 as *Wrinklies' Wit & Wisdom*
This illustrated edition published 2009 by SevenOaks
20 Mortimer Street
London W1T 3JW

Introduction and selection copyright © Rosemarie Jarski 2005
Design copyright © Carlton Publishing Group 2006

10 9 8 7 6

A catalogue record for this book is available from the British Library.

ISBN 978-1-86200-608-9

Typeset by E-Type, Liverpool

The Illustrated

Wrinklies' Wit & Wisdom

Humorous Quotes
About Getting on a Bit

Compiled by Rosemarie Jarski

SEVENOAKS

Contents

Introduction

Last year a company which looks into social trends carried out a survey called 'Understanding Fiftysomethings'. Seventeen hundred people, ranging in age from 45 to 89, were questioned about all aspects of their lives. Part of the research invited participants to send in a photograph, 'a snapshot of your life'. On the cover of the final report was a picture of a wheelchair and a Zimmer frame with these words: 'Among 600 snaps taken by older Britons, we found just one like this. So why is it one of the first images to spring to mind when someone mentions old age?' Pictures submitted included a pair of cowboy boots, a computer, a brochure for hip hotels, a pair of Gina high heels, a bottle of wine, and several packets of Rowntree's jelly.

What this reveals – beyond the pleasing fact that a love of jelly lingers on into one's dotage – is the sheer diversity of older people today. Traditional stereotypes of knitting grannies and doddering grandpas just aren't true anymore (if, indeed, they ever were). Older people dress up, drink wine, travel, surf the net, send texts, have sex. The baby-boomer generation has redefined the meaning of 'old'. Grey is the new black!

Saga-louts are the new lager-louts! Old is the new young!

Or is it?

Old myths die hard. Senior citizens may have changed but the rest of society has yet to notice. The clichéd image of old age is still common currency in our culture. Media and advertising (run by tots barely free of nappy-rash) still lump all older people into one homogenous group. This group is then routinely mocked, trivialized, patronized, or ignored altogether. The over-60s represent over 20 per cent of the population but they feature in only 9 per cent of advertisements and television coverage. The charity Age Concern ran a billboard poster showing the head of a grey-haired man with the caption: 'Ignore this poster. It's got grey hair'. Newspapers and magazines are littered with insidious remarks that undermine or belittle older people. Casual comments like, 'she's on the wrong side of 50', 'he may be in his 60s but …', 'he's still going strong, despite his being 56' may seem innocuous, but multiply them by hundreds of similar comments day after day and they add up to one thing: ageism.

Ageism is entrenched in our society. In

the National Health Service, younger patients are up to twice as likely as older ones to receive the best available treatment. Older patients are also more likely to get a DNR – 'Do Not Resuscitate'. The charity Age Concern highlighted the case of an elderly lady who died in hospital and was found to have NFR ('Not For Resuscitation') written across her toes. If this was racism or sexism there would be riots on the streets and questions in Parliament, but because it's 'only old folk' such scandalous treatment elicits barely more than a raised eyebrow.

The test of a civilized society is how it treats its older citizens. 'It is easy to love children,' writes Abraham Heschel, 'even tyrants and dictators make a point of being fond of children. But the affection and care for the old, the incurable, the helpless are the true gold mines of a culture.' In the United Kingdom, twice as many people give to charities that help animals as those who give to charities supporting older people.

To find respect and deference towards age you have to look beyond Western culture to Asian and African nations. Margaret Simey, a suffragette in the 1920s and local councillor for more than 20 years, was shocked and dismayed to discover that after her retirement she was slung out onto the scrap heap by society and became a non-person. Then she paid a visit to her son in the Southern African kingdom of Lesotho: 'I found myself greeted with enthusiasm by the villagers. Pleased but baffled by my reception, I was told on inquiry that what moved them was their pleasure that my son should enjoy the exceptional good fortune of having such an old mother. To them, my experience and wisdom were worth more than money in the bank.' The Third World has much to teach us about the Third Age.

Similarly, in Japan, reverence for old age is ingrained in their culture and their psyche. As Barbara Bloom observes: 'When the Japanese mend broken objects they aggrandize the damage by filling the cracks with gold, because they believe that when something's suffered damage and has a history it becomes more beautiful.'

Any society that doesn't value its older citizens is off its rocker. We're all getting older so ageism is like turkeys voting for Christmas. Ignorance and fear are at the root of it. Dread of our own deterioration and mortality leads to fear and revulsion of old people who are reminders of that inevitability.

Making role models of celebrities does not help. None fear the ageing process more than they. Celebrities may pay collagen-enhanced-lip-service to growing old gracefully, but then they sneak off to the plastic surgeon's to be nipped, tucked and liposuctioned to within an inch of their livers. They line up to go on Oprah to share their drink, drug and sex addictions but how many will 'fess up to a facelift? There's a saying in Hollywood: 'The second worst sin is to be old; the worst is to look old.' The mother of Zsa Zsa Gabor was still having cosmetic surgery in her 90s. Before going under the knife she instructed her surgeon to complete the procedure even if she died on the operating table.

Let's face it, when it comes to ageing, our society needs to fundamentally rethink its attitudes – and fast. Advances in preventative medicine and improved nutrition mean we're staying healthy and living longer. By 2030, one third of the entire population of the UK will be over 60. Centenarians are the world's fastest-growing age group, and scientists predict that millennium babies can expect to live to be 130.

Great news. But what's the point of these extra years if all we can look forward to are discrimination, derision and yet more adverts for life insurance ('no medical, and no salesman will call')? Life is not just about staying alive but living. What we need are better role models, less hypocrisy, more honesty, an end to the obsession with youth, an education programme to teach the younger generation to value experience and wisdom, and a more accurate reflection of what life is like after the free bus pass.

A collection of wrinklies' wit and wisdom can't change the world; the best it can do is to fly the flag for wrinklies everywhere. Gilded youth is swept aside as golden oldies take centre-stage. But that's not to say that the young can't also find enjoyment – and enlightenment – here. This is a book for anyone who's getting older. John Mortimer, The Golden Girls, Barry Cryer, Bill Cosby and Elaine Stritch are inspirational role models for any age. They never pass their amuse-by dates, their wisdom is timeless. Most of the contributors can ride the buses for free so they speak with the voice of experience. They shoot from the hip – real or titanium – sharing the pleasures as well as what Byron called 'the woes that wait on age'. Wrapping those woes in wit doesn't make them go away but it does make them a bit more bearable. If laughter is the best medicine, consider this the perfect prescription for ageing well and living a full and happy life. Pop a few pearls of wit and wisdom every day and that telegram from Her Majesty is practically in the bag. You see, he who laughs, lasts.

Age is Just a Number

I'm very pleased to be here. Let's face it, at my age I'm pleased to be anywhere.

George Burns

He was either a man of about 150 who was rather young for his years, or a man of about 110 who had been aged by trouble.

P.G. Wodehouse

I'm as old as my tongue and a little bit older than my teeth.

Kris Kringle, **Miracle on 34th Street**

Age is a question of mind over matter. If you don't mind, age don't matter.

Satchel Paige

We're obsessed with age. Numbers are always and pointlessly attached to every name that's published in a newspaper: 'Joe Creamer, 43, and his daughter, Tiffany-Ann, 9, were chasing a bunny, 2, when Tiffany-Ann tripped on the root of a tree, 106.'

Joan Rivers

Let's just say I reached the age of consent 75,000 consents ago.

Shelley Winters

People who define themselves by their age are about as appealing to be with as feminists who drone on about women's rights, homosexuals who are obsessed with being gay, or environmentalists who mention recycling every time they drop by for green tea.

Marcelle D'Argy-Smith

Exactly how old is Joan Collins? We need an expert. Someone who counts the rings on trees.

Ruby Wax

My sister, Jackie, is younger than me. We don't know quite by how much.

Joan Collins

I don't know how old I am because the goat ate the Bible that had my birth certificate in it. The goat lived to be 27.

Satchel Paige

Age is something that doesn't matter, unless you are a cheese.

Billie Burke

Age only matters when one is ageing. Now that I have arrived at a great age, I might just as well be 20.

Pablo Picasso

I'm 80, but in my own mind, my age veers. When I'm performing on stage, I'm 40; when I'm shopping in Waitrose, I'm 120.

Humphrey Lyttelton

I'm 42 around the chest, 52 around the waist, 92 around the golf course and a nuisance around the house.

Groucho Marx

When I turned 2 I was really anxious, because I'd doubled my age in a year. I thought, if this keeps up, by the time I'm 6 I'll be 90.

Steven Wright

How old would you be if you didn't know how old you were?

Satchel Paige

I have no romantic feelings about age. Either you are interesting at any age or you are not. There is nothing particularly interesting about being old – or being young, for that matter.

Katharine Hepburn

'When I was your age …' No one is ever anyone else's age, except physically.

Faith Baldwin

It is a sobering thought that when Mozart was my age he had been dead for two years.

Tom Lehrer

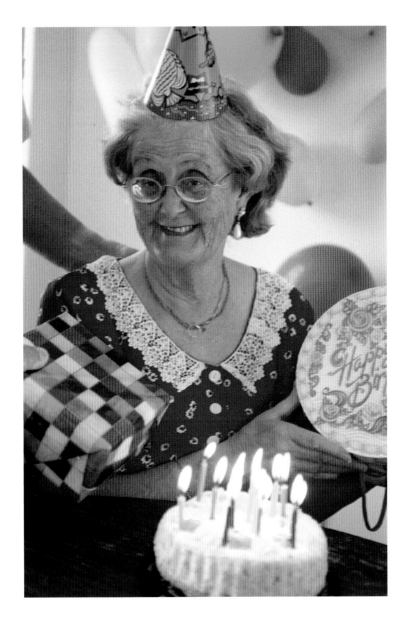

Happy Birthday to You?

Two weeks ago we celebrated my uncle's 103rd birthday. 103
– isn't that something? Unfortunately he wasn't present. How
could he be? He died when he was 29.

Victor Borge

Like a hole in the head I need another birthday.

Dorothy Parker

For all the advances in medicine, there is still no cure for the
common birthday.

John Glenn

A diplomat is a man who always remembers a woman's birthday
but never remembers her age.

Robert Frost

Birthdays are nature's way of telling us to eat more cake.

Jo Brand

Birthdays are good for you. Statistics show that the people who
have the most live the longest.

Larry Lorenzoni

The seven ages of man have become preschooler, Pepsi generation, baby boomer, mid-lifer, empty-nester, senior citizen, and organ donor.

Bill Cosby

The three ages of man: youth, middle age, and 'You're looking wonderful!'

Dore Schary

There are three stages of man: he believes in Santa Claus; he does not believe in Santa Claus; he is Santa Claus.

Bob Phillips

Your 40s, you grow a little potbelly, you grow another chin. The music starts to get too loud and one of your old girlfriends from high school becomes a grandmother. Your 50s you have a minor surgery. You'll call it a procedure, but it's a surgery. Your 60s you have a major surgery, the music is still loud but it doesn't matter because you can't hear it anyway. 70s, you and the wife retire to Fort Lauderdale, you start eating dinner at 2, lunch around 10, breakfast the night before. And you spend most of your time wandering around malls looking for the ultimate in soft yoghurt and muttering 'How come the kids don't call?' By your 80s, you've had a major stroke, and you end up babbling to some Jamaican nurse who your wife can't stand but who you call mama. Any questions?

Mitch Robbins, City Slickers

My mother used to say the seven ages were: childhood, adolescence, adulthood, middle age, elderly, old, and wonderful.

Mary Wilson

I think the life cycle is all backwards. You should die first, get it out of the way. Then you live in an old age home. You get kicked out when you're too young, you get a gold watch, you go to work. You work 40 years until you're young enough to enjoy your retirement. You do drugs, alcohol, you party, you get ready for high school. You go to grade school, you become a kid, you play, you have no responsibilities, you become a little baby, you go back into the womb, you spend your last 9 months floating … and you finish off as an orgasm.

George Carlin

Be on the alert to recognize your prime at whatever time of your life it may occur.

Miss Jean Brodie, **The Prime of Miss Jean Brodie,** *Muriel Spark*

It has begun to occur to me that life is a stage I'm going through.

Ellen Goodman

There are only three ages for women in Hollywood: Babe, District Attorney, and Driving Miss Daisy.

Goldie Hawn

Growing Old

– You know what the worst part about getting old is?
– Your face?

Blanche Devereaux and Dorothy Zbornak, The Golden Girls

Growing old is like being increasingly penalized for a crime you haven't committed.

Anthony Powell

Age to women is like Kryptonite to Superman.

Kathy Lette

There is absolutely nothing to be said in favour of growing old. There ought to be legislation against it.

Patrick Moore

In the middle of the 19th century, an Englishman named Robert Browning wrote: 'Grow old along with me, the best is yet to be.' Clearly this man was a minor poet. Or else he wrote those lines when he was 12.

Joan Rivers

I am not 'of a certain age', Niles. I am smack dab in the middle of 'not a kid anymore'. I won't be 'of a certain age' for another 10 years.

Frasier Crane, **Frasier**

Frasier, you may think it's tough being middle aged but think about me – I've got a son who's middle aged.

Martin Crane, **Frasier**

Middle age is when you're sitting at home on Saturday night and the telephone rings and you hope it isn't for you.

Ogden Nash

I am at that age. Too young for the bowling green, too old for Ecstasy.

Rab C. Nesbitt

One problem with growing older is that it gets increasingly tougher to find a famous historical figure who didn't amount to much when he was your age.

Bill Vaughan

There are days of oldness, and then one gets young again. It goes backward and forward, not in one direction.

Katharine Hathaway

When the Pope Starts Looking Young

SIGNS YOU'RE GETTING OLD

I've started wearing cardigans and saying things like 'Whoopsadaisy', and when I take a first sip of tea, 'Ooh, that hits the spot!'

Gary, Men Behaving Badly

If, at the age of 30, you are stiff and out of shape, then you are old. If, at 60, you are supple and strong, then you are young.

Joseph Pilates

Signs you're getting on a bit: your back hurts; you eat food past its sell-by date; your carpet is patterned; you go supermarket shopping in the evening to pick up marked-down bargains; you can spell; you hang your clothes on padded coat hangers; you save the hearing aid flyer that falls out of the colour supplement; you try to get electrical gadgets repaired when they go wrong; you save the free little packets of sugar from cafés; you have worn a knitted swimsuit; when you watch black and white films you spend the whole time pointing at the screen going, 'He's dead … She's dead …'; your car stereo is tuned to Radio 2.

Colin Slater

You know you're getting older if you have more fingers
than real teeth.

Rodney Dangerfield

One of the signs of old age is that you have to carry your senses
around in your handbag – glasses, hearing aid, dentures, etc.

Kurt Strauss

I contemplated buying a new cream that claimed to stop the 7
signs of ageing and wondered what they might be. Incontinence?
Talking about the weather? Wearing slippers? Memory loss?
Compulsive need to queue up at the post office? Memory loss?
Inability to comprehend the lyrics of pop songs?

Maria McErlane

I first felt old walking in Spain with my 13-year-old daughter
when I belatedly realized the wolf-whistle was not for me.

Adele Thorpe

I know I must be getting old because I saw a young lady with her
midriff showing and thought, 'Ooh, you must be cold.'

John Marsh

You know you're knocking on when you get to the top of the
stairs and can't remember what you went up for. So you go back
downstairs to help you remember what you went upstairs for. You

finally remember what you went upstairs for so up you go again but when you find it you have forgotten why you wanted it.
Millicent Kemp

You know you're getting older when the first thing you do after you're done eating is look for a place to lie down.
Louie Anderson

A young boy down the road tried to help me across the road this afternoon. I gave him a swift cuff round the ear. Only be a matter of time before they're forcing me on a day trip to Eastbourne.
Victor Meldrew, **One Foot in the Grave**

You know you're getting old when you go on holiday and always pack a sweater.
Denis Norden

You know you're getting old when you feel like the day after the night before and you haven't even been anywhere.
Milton Berle

You're getting old when you stop loving snow and sweetcorn.
Susan H. Llewellyn

You know you're getting old when you and your partner wear matching sweaters.
Mark Schofield

Old Age

At a church social, a little boy came up and asked me how old I was. I said, 'I'm 76.' 'And you're still alive?' he said.

Jack Wilson

Alive in the sense that he can't legally be buried.

Geoffrey Madan

– Smithers, what's my password?
– It's your age, sir.
– Excellent! [4 beeps are heard]

Mr Burns and Smithers, **The Simpsons**

– I'm a college professor. What did you think when I said I taught Hemingway?
– I thought you were old.

Miles Webber and Rose Martin, **The Golden Girls**

I'm so old that when I order a 3-minute egg, they ask for the money up front.

Milton Berle

I'm so old I daren't even buy green bananas.

Bruce Forsyth

I'm at an age when if I drop a fiver in the collection plate, it's not a donation, it's an investment.

Ralph Layton

Anyone can get old. All you have to do is to live long enough.

Groucho Marx

How do you know when you're old? When you double your current age and realize you're not going to live that long.

Michael Leyden

I'm 59 and people call me middle aged. How many 118-year-old men do you know?

Barry Cryer

Old age is like waiting in the departure lounge of life. Fortunately, we are in England and the train is bound to be late.

Milton Shulman

You are as young as your faith, as old as your doubt; as young as your self-confidence, as old as your fear; as young as your hope, as old as your despair.

Douglas MacArthur

I hope I never get so old I get religious.

Ingmar Bergman

Old age is not for sissies.

Bette Davis

I don't know how you feel about old age, but in my case I didn't even see it coming. It hit me from the rear.

Phyllis Diller

The ageing process is not gradual or gentle. It rushes up, pushes you over and runs off laughing. Dying is a matter of slapstick and prat falls.

John Mortimer

Old age is like underwear. It creeps up on you.

Lois L. Kaufman

Old age is the most unexpected of all things that happen to a man.

Leon Trotsky

A person is always startled when he hears himself called an old man for the first time.

Oliver Wendell Holmes

I do what I can to help the elderly; after all, I'm going to be old myself some day.

Lillian Carter, 76

Appearance

– Good afternoon, I'm Dorothy Zbornak.
– Geriatrics is two doors down on the left.

***Dorothy Zbornak and Hospital Receptionist,* Empty Nest**

There is a saying, 'Youth is a gift of nature; Age is a work of art.' If age is a work of art, the artist is one who belongs on the subway and not in the Louvre.

Bill Cosby

As I rose from my bath, I caught sight of myself in the mirror. I suddenly saw a great white sea monster emerging out of the water. This enormous sub-aquatic creature could not possibly be me, could it?

Julian Fellowes

I still think of myself as I was 25 years ago. Then I look in the mirror and see an old bastard and I realize it's me.

Dave Allen

Let us be grateful to the mirror for revealing to us our appearance only.

Samuel Butler

It is 11 years since I have seen my figure in a mirror: the last reflection I saw there was so disagreeable I resolved to spare myself such mortification in the future, and shall continue that resolution to my life's end.

Lady Mary Wortley Montagu

Sometimes I catch a glimpse of my outward self reflected in a shop window and see my mother. That old woman can't be me!

Prue Phillipson

A while ago I asked John Clarke to give us a talk here at Knapely Women's Institute. Annie asked me to read it to you here tonight, and this is what he wrote: 'The flowers of Yorkshire are like the women of Yorkshire. Every stage of their growth has its own beauty, but the last phase is always the most glorious. Then very quickly they all go to seed.'

Chris, **Calendar Girls**

If you really want to annoy your glamorous, well-preserved 42 year-old auntie, say, 'I bet you were really pretty when you were young.'

Lily Savage

Twenty-four years ago, Madam, I was incredibly handsome. The remains of it are still visible through the rift of time. I was so handsome that women became spellbound when I came in view.

In San Francisco, in rainy seasons, I was frequently mistaken for a cloudless day.

Mark Twain

After a certain number of years, our faces become our biographies.

Cynthia Ozick

Eric Sykes is about to be 79. He has the stretching, slowly inquiring, slightly doomy head of one of those lovely, ancient sea turtles you see on wildlife programmes.

Deborah Ross

An old man looks permanent, as if he had been born an old man.

H.E. Bates

I have reached the age when I look just as good standing on my head as I do right side up.

Frank Sullivan

Jesus! Look at my hands. Now really, I am too young for liver spots. Maybe I can merge them into a tan.

Diane, **September**

I swear I'm ageing about as well as a beach-party movie.

Harvey Fierstein, **Torch Song Trilogy**

Dress

Dorothy, was Sophia naked just now or does her dress really need ironing?

Rose Nylund, The Golden Girls

Men in the uniform of Wall Street retirement: black Chesterfield coat, rimless glasses and The Times folded to the obituary page.

Jimmy Breslin

Inspired by the line in Jenny Joseph's poem 'Warning' that vows, 'When I am an old woman, I shall wear purple, with a red hat that doesn't go', I started 'The Red Hat Society'. It's for women who want to grow old playfully.

Sue Ellen Cooper

Never wear grey. Wearing grey makes one feel grey. I was shown round Tutankhamun's tomb in the 1920s. I saw all this wonderful pink on the walls and the artefacts. I was so impressed that I vowed to wear it for the rest of my life.

Barbara Cartland

– Dorothy, do you think I'm dressed okay for the dog races?
– That depends – are you competing?

Blanche Devereaux and Sophia Petrillo, The Golden Girls

My mother buys me those big granny panties, 3 in a pack.
You can use them for a car cover.

Monique Marvez

Caesar had his toga, Adam had his leaf, but when I wear a thong it
gives my piles such grief.

Sandra Mayhew

My dad's trousers kept creeping up on him. By the time he was 65,
he was just a pair of pants and a head.

Jeff Altman

I have never seen an old person in a new bathing suit in my life.
I don't know where they get their bathing suits, but my father
has bathing suits from other centuries. If I forget mine, he always
wants me to wear his.

Jerry Seinfeld

I'm a child of the Sixties. I still wear jeans and yes, my bum looks
big in them but then my bum looked big in 1965.

Julia Richardson

I can see nothing wrong with 40-, 50-, or 60-year-old men
dressing and acting like teenagers. I'm an elderly man of 44 and,
after a few miserable years of being sensible, I do it all the time.

Jeremy Clarkson

A sign your best years are behind you is when you slip into your first pair of slippers. They smack of smugness and a grisly domesticity.

Piers Hernu

Roll carpet slippers in breadcrumbs, bake until golden brown, then tell friends you're wearing Findus Crispy Pancakes.

H. Lloyd, 'Top Tip', Viz magazine

At 50, confine your piercings to sardine cans.

Joan Rivers

– Now, if you'll excuse me, I'm going to slip into something that will make me look my best.
– May I suggest a time-machine?

Blanche Devereaux and Sophia Petrillo, **The Golden Girls**

Hair Today, Gone Tomorrow

I found my first grey hair today. On my chest.

Wendy Liebman

A wonderful woman my grandmother – 86 years old and not a single grey hair on her head. She's completely bald.

Les Dawson

When men get grey hair, they look distinguished. When women get grey hair, they look old. When women get breasts, they look sexy. When men get breasts, they look old.

Dick Solomon

Grey-haired men look 'distinguished'? Surely the word is 'extinguished'.

Julie Burchill

– Hi Stan. Where's your hair?
– Oh damn, I should never have left the sun roof down.

Rose Nylund and Stan Zbornak, **The Golden Girls**

I used to think I'd like less grey hair. Now I'd like more of it.

Richie Benaud

I knew I was going bald when it was taking longer and longer to wash my face.

Harry Hill

The method preferred by most balding men for making themselves look silly is called the 'comb-over', which is when the man grows the hair on one side of his head very long and combs it across the bald area, creating an effect that looks from the top like an egg in the grasp of a large tropical spider.

Dave Barry

Men going bald is Nature's way of stopping them having any more crap hairstyles.

Tony, **Men Behaving Badly**

Peter Stringfellow's hairstyle is older than some of his girlfriends.

Paul Merton

There's one good thing about being bald: it's neat.

Milton Berle

The most delightful advantage of being bald – one can hear snowflakes.

R.G. Daniels

I love bald men. Just because you've lost your fuzz doesn't mean you ain't a peach.

Dolly Parton

Over the years, I've tried a variety of ways to regain my hair. I had shots of oestrogen in my scalp. I didn't grow any hair – but I went up a cup size.

Tony Kornheiser

– Do you think she's wearing a wig?
– Yes, definitely, but it's a very good one. You'd never guess.

Two old ladies overheard on a bus

People ask me how long it takes to do my hair. I don't know, I'm never there.

Dolly Parton

The hair is real. It's the head that's fake.

Steve Allen

His toupee makes him look 20 years sillier.

Bill Dana

If that thing had legs it'd be a rat.

Martin Kemp

Eat, Drink and Be Merry ...

As I get older, I'm trying to eat healthy. I've got Gordon Ramsay's new cook book, Take Two Eggs and F★★★ Off.

Jack Dee

Joan Collins says you are what you eat. She reached this conclusion following experiences in the swinging sixties and is very careful about what she puts in her mouth these days.

Mrs Merton

I'm at the age when food has taken the place of sex in my life. In fact, I've just had a mirror put over my kitchen table.

Rodney Dangerfield

Gin is a dangerous drink. It's clear and innocuous looking. You also have to be 45, female and sitting on the stairs.

Dylan Moran

I'll tell you what I haven't seen for a long time: my testicles.

John Sparkes

I've gained a few pounds around the middle. The only lower-body garments I own that still fit me comfortably are towels.

Dave Barry

I don't have a beer belly. It's a Burgundy belly and it cost me a lot of money.

Charles Clarke

You can only hold your stomach in for so many years.

Burt Reynolds

Weighing scales are usually accurate, but never tactful.

Bill Cosby

I had to go to the doctor's last week. He told me to take all my clothes off. Then he said, 'You'll have to diet.' I said, 'What colour?'

Ken Dodd

I'm on a new diet – Viagra and prune juice. I don't know if I'm coming or going.

Rodney Dangerfield

Why is it all the things I like eating have been proven to cause tumours in white mice?

Robert Benchley

Welcome to the Wonderful World of 70: The Oat Bran Years.

Denis Norden

Exercise

You gotta stay in shape. My grandmother started walking 5 miles a day when she was 60. She's 97 today and we don't know where the hell she is.

Ellen DeGeneres

I get up at 7am each day to do my exercises – after I have first put on my make-up. After all, La Loren is always La Loren.

Sophia Loren, 70

I exercise every morning without fail. Up, down! Up, down! And then the other eyelid.

Phyllis Diller

I swim a lot. It's either that or buy a new golf ball.

Bob Hope

I keep fit. Every morning, I do 100 laps of an Olympic-sized swimming pool – in a small motor launch.

Peter Cook

Police in Norway stopped Sigrid Krohn de Lange running down the street in Bergen because they thought that she had escaped from a nursing home. The 94-year-old jogger was out getting fit.

The Irish Independent

My doctor recently told me that jogging could add years to my life. I think he was right. I feel 10 years older already.

Milton Berle

The only reason I would take up jogging is so I could hear heavy breathing again.

Erma Bombeck

Go jogging? What, and get hit by a meteor?

Robert Benchley

The doctor asked me if I ever got breathless after exercise. I said no, never, because I never exercise.

John Mortimer

I am pushing 60. That is enough exercise for me.

Mark Twain

To get back my youth, I would do anything in the world, except take exercise, get up early, or be respectable.

Oscar Wilde

Whenever I get the urge to exercise, I lie down until the feeling passes away.

Robert M. Hutchins

Showbiz and Hollywood

I am in an industry where they eat their elders.

Dale Winton

In Los Angeles, by the time you're 35, you're older than most of the buildings.

Delia Ephron

Actress years seem like dog years and that makes me about 266.

Sharon Stone

I can't think of anything grimmer than being an ageing actress – God! It's worse than being an ageing homosexual.

Candice Bergen

You have to be born a sex symbol. You don't become one. If you're born with it, you'll have it even when you're 100 years old.

Sophia Loren

In Hollywood, great-grandmothers dread growing old.

Phyllis Batelli

Oscar time is my busiest season. I'm like an accountant during the tax season.

Richard Fleming, Beverly Hills plastic surgeon

Arnold Schwarzenegger is getting old. He's changed his catchphrase from 'I'll be back' to 'Oh, my back'.

David Letterman

– You give your age here as 40. I happen to know that you are at least 50.
– Oh no, no, no. I absolutely refuse to count the last 10 years in Hollywood as part of my life.

Reporter and William Meiklejohn

Adam Faith is only 42, but Terry Nelhams is 62.

Adam Faith

I did not expect an Honorary Oscar – well, actually, I did. But not for another 25 years.

Federico Fellini

Awards are like haemorrhoids: in the end every asshole gets one.

Frederic Raphael

Hollywood obits are regularly in the high 80s – these are people who live a long time, which is what happens if you don't smoke, you work out every day, you get your body fat awesomely low and you do only the best cocaine.

David Thomson

Music

The Rolling Stones are on tour again. They were gonna call the tour 'The Rolling Stones Live Plus Keith Richards'.

David Letterman

– What do you think John Lennon would have been like at 64?
– He would be just John – all that he was before. But I think talking about a person's age is ageism, like racism or sexism. It isolates attitudes.

Yoko Ono

The Rolling Stones are on tour again. They were gonna call the tour 'Hey! You! Get Offa My Stairlift!'

David Letterman

I'm always asked, 'What about being too old to rock 'n' roll?' Presumably lots of writers get better as they get older. So why shouldn't I?

Lou Reed

The Rolling Stones are on tour again. They were gonna call the tour 'And You Thought Aerosmith Was Old'.

David Letterman

I can still rock like a son of a bitch.

Ozzy Osbourne

The Rolling Stones are on tour again. They were gonna call the tour 'We Live Through the Concert or Your Money Back'.

David Letterman

The Grateful Dead are like bad architecture or an old whore. Stick around long enough and you eventually get respectable.

Jerry Garcia

The Rolling Stones are on tour again. They were gonna call the tour 'Brown Sugar and Lots of Bran'.

David Letterman

When I give concerts, I ask women not to throw their knickers at me. At my age, I don't want to be a caricature of myself.

Tom Jones

The Rolling Stones are on tour again. They were gonna call the tour 'Under 45s Not Admitted Without a Parent'.

David Letterman

People are always talking about when the Rolling Stones should retire, but it's a racial thing. Nobody ever says B.B. King is too old to play. It's like you can't be white and be an old rock 'n' roller.

David Bailey

Holding Back the Years

Old Father Time will turn you into a hag if you don't show the bitch who's boss.

Mae West

I don't plan to grow old gracefully. I plan to have face-lifts until my ears meet.

Rita Rudner

I see a lot of new faces. Especially on the old faces.

Johnny Carson

In Los Angeles, people don't get older, they just get tighter.

Greg Proops

I've had so much plastic surgery, if I have one more face-lift it will be a caesarean.

Phyllis Diller

I wish I had a twin, so I could know what I'd look like without plastic surgery.

Joan Rivers

Now I'm getting older I take health supplements: geranium,
dandelion, passionflower, hibiscus. I feel great, and when I pee,
I experience the fresh scent of potpourri.

Sheila Wenz

Wrinkle cream doesn't work. I've been using it for two years and
my balls still look like raisins.

Harland Williams

– I gave Maris botox injections as a gift for our wedding
anniversary one year.
– Oh, yes, probably your 10th. That's 'Toxins', isn't it?

Niles and Frasier Crane, **Frasier**

Moisturisers do work. The rest is pap. There is nothing on God's
earth that will take away 30 years of arguing with your husband.

Anita Roddick

Anti-wrinkle cream there may be, but anti-fat-bastard cream there
is not.

Dave, **The Full Monty**

The best anti-ageing cream is ice cream. What other food makes
you feel like you're 8 years old again?

Anon

The Fountain of Youth

My recipe for perpetual youth? I've never had my face in the sun, and I have a very handsome young husband … Sex is one of the best and cheapest beauty treatments there is.

Joan Collins

The secret of my youthful appearance is simply mashed swede. As a face-mask, as a night-cap, and in an emergency, as a draught-excluder.

Kitty, Victoria Wood

Jewellery takes people's minds off your wrinkles.

Sonja Henie

Jewellery should be bold. Neat little pearls can add 10 years.

Joan Collins

If you don't want to get old, don't mellow.

Linda Ellerbee

To have the respect of my peers and the admiration of young people beats plastic surgery any day.

Johnny Cash

The fountain of youth is a mixture of gin and vermouth.

Cole Porter

With them I'm Jack Nicholson. Without them I'm fat and 60.

Jack Nicholson on his trademark sunglasses

You're only as young as the last time you changed your mind.

Timothy Leary

It's very ageing to talk about age.

Merle Oberon

There is a fountain of youth: it is your mind, your talents, the creativity you bring to your life and to the lives of the people you love.

Sophia Loren

An inordinate passion for pleasure is the secret of remaining young.

Oscar Wilde

People are living longer because of the decline in religion. Not many people believe in the hereafter, so they keep going.

Cyril Clarke

One of the secrets of a long and fruitful life is to forgive everybody everything every night before you go to bed.

Bernard M. Baruch

I have only managed to live so long by carrying no hatreds.
Winston Churchill

Old people who shine from inside look 10 to 20 years younger.
Dolly Parton

As long as you can still be disappointed, you are still young.
Sarah Churchill

Whatever a man's age, he can reduce it several years by putting a bright-coloured flower in his buttonhole.
Mark Twain

At my age flowers scare me.
George Burns

If you want to stay young-looking, pick your parents very carefully.
Dick Clark

The secret of salvation in old age is this: keep sweet, keep useful, and keep busy.
Elbert Hubbard

The secret to old age: you have to know what you're going to do the next day.
Louis J. Lefkowitz

Maturity

You grow up the day you have the first real laugh – at yourself.

Ethel Barrymore

The first sign of maturity is the disco very that the volume knob also turns to the left.

Jerry Wright

You know you've grown up when you become obsessed with the thermostat.

Jeff Foxworthy

What I look forward to is continued immaturity followed by death.

Dave Barry

Age is a very high price to pay for maturity.

Tom Stoppard

Tony Benn immatures with age.

Harold Wilson

No one is ever old enough to know better.

Holbrook Jackson

Act Your Age

The older you get, the more important it is not to act your age.
Ashleigh Brilliant

We don't stop playing because we grow old, we grow old because we stop playing.
George Bernard Shaw

I've always believed the secret of eternal youth is arrested development.
Alice Roosevelt Longworth

The ageing process has you firmly in its grasp if you never get the urge to throw a snowball.
Doug Larson

Even though I'm very old, I always feel like the youngest person in the room.
W.H. Auden

To be young, really young, takes a very long time.
Pablo Picasso

The great man is one who never loses his child's heart.
Mencius

I'm Not Menthyl

MALAPROPISMS

My nan, God bless 'er, gets things a bit mixed up. She said to me the other day, 'I've bought one of those new George Formby grills.'

Peter Kay

– Barbara, didn't Elsie next door have implants?
– No, eggplants, Mam.

Nana and Barbara Royle, **The Royle Family**

My mother thinks a crouton is a Japanese sofa.

Mary Unfaithful

– He's autistic, Gran.
– That's nice. I wish I could draw.

Martin and Millicent Smith

Our Susan's still not had her baby. If she doesn't have it soon she'll have to be seduced.

Brenda Sneddon

Mark my words: her chickens will come home to roast.

Coral Greene

My mum said, 'I saw whatsaname last week, oh, whatshisname,
I can never remember anything these days – it's this damned
anorexia.'

Stephen Fry

I can't be doin' with Donny Osmond and that bunch of Morons.

Bert Fletcher

My nan was complaining of chest pains. I said, 'Are you all right,
Nan?' She said, 'I think I've got vagina.'

Peter Kay

Oh, love, can you get me some of that cunnilinctus for my cough?

Edna Steele

I've got bigger fish to fly!

Elsie Mason

The patio doors are sticking again. Have you got some of that UB40?

Phyllis Amison

The doctor says I have to have a hearing aid because there's a
blockage in my Euston station tube.

Joe Hadley

I don't want to see a pieciatrist; I'm not menthyl!

Hylda Baker, **Nearest and Dearest**

Pleasures and Perks of Growing Older

As you grow old, you lose interest in sex, your friends drift away, and your children often ignore you. There are other advantages, of course, but these are the outstanding ones.

Richard Needham

– You know the best thing about being old?
– Cardigans?
– No. Disabled parking spaces.

Anon

One compensation of old age is that it excuses you from picnics.

William Feather

One of the delights of being a senior citizen is it's easy to annoy young people. Step 1: get in the car. Step 2: turn the indicator on. Step 3: leave it on for 50 miles.

David Letterman

I can't wait to get old enough to ride in one of those buggies at the airport. Whizzing past all those poor sods on the long trek to the departure gate. It will make being old worthwhile.

Sean Needham

One good thing about being old and having a failing memory is that I can enjoy the endless repeats of programmes like *Inspector Morse, Murder She Wrote,* and *Midsomer Murders* because I can never remember whodunit.

Larry Simpkins

One of the good things about getting older is that you find you're more interesting than most of the people you meet.

Lee Marvin

I basically enjoy getting older because I get smarter. So what I have to say is more worth listening to, in my opinion.

Clive James

I used to dread getting older because I thought I would not be able to do all the things I wanted to do, but now that I am older I find that I don't want to do them.

Nancy Astor, 80

One of the delights known to age, and beyond the grasp of youth, is that of Not Going.

J.B. Priestley

By the by, as I must leave off being young, I find many Douceurs in being a sort of Chaperon for I am put on the Sofa near the fire and can drink as much wine as I like.

Jane Austen

My husband's idea of a good night out is a good night in.

Maureen Lipman

I think happiness is easier to come by when you're older: Go for a nice walk and do some push-ups. Sex is always good. A hamburger will work, if you make it right and make it yourself. It should be rare and have raw onion and a lot of mustard. A martini, just one, is really fabulous. Going to Mass on Sunday morning, if it is the right sort of Mass, when the homily is short and the choir hangs together just right … Sleep. Sleep is always good. You almost always feel better when you wake up. Baseball games. And Louis Armstrong …

Garrison Keillor

One of the many pleasures of old age is giving things up.

Malcolm Muggeridge

I always make a point of starting the day at 6 a.m. with champagne. It goes straight to the heart and cheers one up. White wine won't do. You need the bubbles.

John Mortimer

Pottering is the most fun you can have in slippers.

Guy Browning

If I'm feeling really wild I don't bother flossing before bedtime.

Judith Viorst

The great thing about being in your 70s is, what can they do to you? What have you got to lose? Freedom is just another word for having nothing left to lose.

Clint Eastwood

As a man grows older it is harder and harder to frighten him.

Jean Paul Richter

All one's life as a young woman one is on show. You set yourself up to be noticed and admired. And then, not expecting it, you become middle-aged, anonymous. No one notices you. You achieve a wonderful freedom. You can move about, unnoticed and invisible.

Doris Lessing

Bored? Here's a way the over-50 set can easily kill a good half hour: 1) Place your car keys in your right hand. 2) With your left hand call a friend and confirm a lunch or dinner date. 3) Hang up the phone. 4) Now look for your car keys.

Steve Martin

Now I'm getting older, I don't need to do drugs anymore. I can get the same effect just by standing up real fast.

Jonathan Katz

The older you get, the better you get – unless you're a banana.

Anon

My kitchen linoleum is so black and shiny that I waltz while I wait for the kettle to boil. This pleasure is for the old who live alone.

Florida Scott-Maxwell

A few perks of old age: things I buy now won't wear out; I enjoy hearing arguments about pensions; my secrets are safe with my friends because they can't remember them either.

Felicity Muir

There's nothing like a flutter on the horses for a bit of excitement. Might raise the blood pressure but not as threatening as nicotine and alcohol.

Dorothy Norton

The nice thing about being old is that it doesn't affect your betting; in fact, old people betting makes more sense than young people betting. The lady in the bookie's said to me, 'Do you like having a little bet?' I told her no, I loathed it. I like to make big bets.

Clement Freud

One of my pleasures is to read in bed every night a few pages of P.G. Wodehouse, so that if I die in my sleep it will be with a smile on my face.

Arthur Marshall

One of the advantages of being 70 is that you need only 4 hours' sleep. True, you need it 4 times a day, but still.

Denis Norden

One good thing about getting older is that if you're getting married, the phrase 'till death do you part' doesn't sound so horrible. It only means about 10 or 15 years and not the eternity it used to mean.

Joy Behar

One of the greatest pleasures of growing old is looking back at the people you didn't marry.

Elizabeth Taylor

One of the pleasures of age is to find out that one was right, and that one was much righter than one knew at say 17 or 23.

Ezra Pound

The joy of being older is that in one's life one can, towards the end of the run, overact appallingly.

Quentin Crisp

Given 3 requisites – means of existence, reasonable health, and an absorbing interest – those years beyond 60 can be the happiest and most satisfying of a lifetime.

Earnest Calkins

Pick More Daisies

REGRETS

−You're now 76 years old. Do you have any regrets in life?
−Yes, I haven't had enough sex.

Interviewer and John Betjeman

My one regret in life is that I am not someone else.

Woody Allen

My greatest regret is not knowing at 30 what I knew about women at 60.

Arthur Miller

I rather regret I haven't taken more drugs. Is it too late, at 70, to try cocaine? Would it be dangerous or interesting?

Joan Bakewell

If I had my life to live over again, I'd make the same mistakes − only sooner.

Tallulah Bankhead

You know, by the time you reach my age, you've made plenty of mistakes if you've lived your life properly.

Ronald Reagan, 76

The only thing in my life that I regret is that I once saved David Frost from drowning. I had to pull him out, otherwise nobody would have believed I didn't push him in.

Peter Cook

My only regret in life is that I did not drink more champagne.

John Maynard Keynes

If I had my life to live over again, I would do everything the exact same way, with the possible exception of seeing the movie remake of Lost Horizon.

Woody Allen

If I had my life to live over, I would pick more daisies.

Nadine Stair

If I had it all to do over again, I would spend more time with my children. I would make my money before spending it. I would learn the joys of wine instead of hard liquor. I would not smoke cigarettes when I had pneumonia. I would not marry the fifth time.

John Huston

If I had my life to live over, I'd live over a saloon.

W.C. Fields

If I had my life to live over, I don't think I'd have the strength.

Flip Wilson

If I had my life to live over again, I would have cried and laughed less while watching television and more while watching life. I would have sat on the lawn with my children and not worried about grass stains. When my kids kissed me impetuously, I would not have said, 'Later. Now go get washed for dinner.' There would have been more I love you's and more I'm sorry's. I would seize every minute … look at it and really see it … live it … and never give it back.

Erma Bombeck

I regret having been so polite in the past. I'd like to trample on at least a dozen people.

Harold Brodkey

If I have my life to live over again I should form the habit of nightly composing myself to thoughts of death. There is no other practice which so intensifies life.

Muriel Spark

Looking back, I have this to regret, that too often when I loved, I did not say so.

David Grayson

At Least I Have My Health

I've just become a pensioner so I've started saving up for my own hospital trolley.

Tom Baker

The time will come in your life, it will almost certainly come, when the voice of God will thunder at you from a cloud, 'From this day forth thou shalt not be able to put on thine own socks.'

John Mortimer

I feel age like an icicle down my back.

Dyson Carter

When I wake up in the morning and nothing hurts, I know I must be dead.

George Burns

I don't need you to remind me of my age, I have a bladder to do that for me.

Stephen Fry

When you get to my age, life seems little more than one long march to and from the lavatory.

John Mortimer

At 75, I sleep like a log. I never have to get up in the middle of the night to go to the bathroom. I go in the morning. Every morning, like clockwork, at 7am, I pee. Unfortunately, I don't wake up till 8.

Harry Beckworth

Thanks to modern medical advances such as antibiotics, nasal spray and Diet Coke, it has become routine for people in the civilized world to pass the age of 40, sometimes more than once.

Dave Barry

When I was 40, my doctor advised me that a man in his 40s shouldn't play tennis. I heeded his advice carefully and could hardly wait until I reached 50 to start again.

Hugo Black

When I turned 50, I went off to have my prostate checked because I kept reading I should. F★★★★★★ finger up the a★★★, I can do without that again.

Bob Geldof

Now I'm over 50 my doctor says I should go out and get more fresh air and exercise. I said, 'All right, I'll drive with the car window open.'

Angus Walker

– How do you know which pills to take?
– Doesn't make any difference. Whatever they fix, I got.
Oscar Madison and Felix Ungar, The Odd Couple II

My mother is no spring chicken, although she has got as many chemicals in her as one.
Dame Edna Everage

Why do the medical profession still keep writing on prescription bottles in a size that only a 20-year-old can read? You were standing there with the medicine bottle in your hand and you died because you couldn't read the directions.
Bill Cosby

Half the modern drugs could well be thrown out the window, except that the birds might eat them.
Martin H. Fischer

I don't know much about medicine, but I know what I like.
S.J. Perelman

Casey came home from seeing the doctor looking very worried. His wife said, 'What's the problem?' He said, 'The doctor told me I have to take a pill every day for the rest of my life.' She said, 'So what, lots of people have to take a pill every day for the rest of their lives.' He said, 'I know, but he only gave me four.'
Hal Roach

Going Gaga

They say that after the age of 20 you lose 50,000 brain cells a day. I don't believe it. I think it's much more.

Ned Sherrin

A 'senior moment' is a euphemism to indicate a temporary loss of marbles to anyone over 50.

Anon

As you get older, you've probably noticed that you tend to forget things. You'll be talking at a party, and you'll know that you know this person, but no matter how hard you try, you can't remember his or her name. This can be very embarrassing, especially if he or she turns out to be your spouse.

Dave Barry

Remembering something at first try is now as good as an orgasm as far as I'm concerned.

Gloria Steinem

First, you forget names, then you forget faces. Next, you forget to pull your zipper up and finally you forget to pull it down.

Leo Rosenberg

My memory's starting to go. The only thing I still retain is water.

Alex Cole

To my deafness I'm accustomed,
To my dentures I'm resigned,
I can manage my bifocals,
But O, how I miss my mind.

Anon

– Hurry up, Dorothy, we're going to be late for Temple.
– Ma, it's Tuesday and we're Catholic.

Sophia Petrillo and Dorothy Zbornak, **The Golden Girls**

'You are old, Father William,' the young man said,
'And your hair has become very white;
And yet you incessantly stand on your head –
Do you think, at your age, it is right?'
'In my youth,' Father William replied to his son,
'I feared it might injure the brain;
But, now that I'm perfectly sure I have none,
Why, I do it again and again.'

Lewis Carroll

I had always looked on myself as a sort of freak whom age could
not touch, which was where I made the ruddy error, because I'm
really a senile wreck with about one and a half feet in the grave.

P.G. Wodehouse, 69

His golf bag doesn't contain a full set of irons.

Robin Williams

I still have a full deck. I just shuffle slower.

Milton Berle

Spare a thought for my friend Eliza Hamilton, who was wrongly diagnosed as mentally unstable when all she was was a bit giddy.

Mrs Merton

On visiting an old folk's home, the Mayoress said 'Good morning' to one of the residents. She looked a bit puzzled, so the Mayoress said, 'Do you know who I am?' The lady gave her a sympathetic look and said, 'No, dear, but if you ask the matron, she'll tell you.'

Anon

Been There, Done That, Can't Remember.

Slogan on a senior citizen's T-shirt

– Can you remember any of your past lives?
– At my age I have a problem remembering what happened yesterday.

Interviewer and the Dalai Lama

The face is familiar, but I can't remember my name.

Robert Benchley

Grandparents and Grandchildren

Mothers bear children. Grandmothers enjoy them.

Spanish proverb

My daughter pointed out the other day, 'A granny is only a double-decker mummy.'

Jilly Cooper

We are a grandmother.

Margaret Thatcher

I can't be a grandmother. I'm too young. Grandmothers are old. They bake and they sew. I was at Woodstock! I pissed in the fields!

Karen Buckman, **Parenthood**

I don't like the idea of being a 'grandmother' - old and frail and the next person to go to heaven. The result of this created image was that when I go to visit my grandchildren in Liverpool nobody offers to carry my case upstairs, and when someone's car breaks down they send for me to help push it.

Carla Lane

Where have all the grannies gone? I mean the genuine, original, 22-carat articles who wore black shawls and cameo brooches, sat in rocking chairs and smelled of camphor?

Keith Waterhouse

True grannies were never seen in shops. They were never seen anywhere except at funerals. They did not visit their grand-chidren: their grandchildren visited them. They would not have anything to do with electricity – true grannies were gas driven.

Keith Waterhouse

Becoming a grandmother is great fun because you can use the kid to get back at your daughter.

Roseanne

Grandchildren don't make me feel old. It's the knowledge that I'm married to a grandmother.

Norman Collie

Grampa Simpson: Favourite Pastimes: napping, collecting beef jerky, sending complaint letters to newspapers and politicians, going to Herman's Military Antiques Store.

The Simpsons

Perfect love sometimes does not come till the first grandchild.

Welsh proverb

What feeling in all the world is so nice as that of a child's hand in yours? What tenderness it arouses, what power it conjures. You are instantly the very touchstone of wisdom and strength.

Marjorie Holmes

The reason grandparents and grandchildren get along so well is that they have a common enemy.

Sam Levenson

Never have children, only grandchildren.

Gore Vidal

Every generation revolts against its fathers and makes friends with its grandfathers.

Lewis Mumford

It's funny that those things your kids did that got on your nerves seem so cute when your grandchildren do them.

Raymond Holland

Does Grandpa love to babysit his grandchildren? Are you kidding? By day he is too busy taking hormone shots at the doctor's or chip shots on the golf course. At night he and Grandma are too busy doing the cha-cha.

Hal Boyle

Grandparents Observed

My husband and I have decided to start a family while my parents are still young enough to look after them.

Rita Rudner

My grandmother was a very tough woman. She buried three husbands. Two of them were just napping.

Rita Rudner

Grandmother, as she gets older, is not fading, but becoming more concentrated.

Paulette Alden

I was talking to my nan about Ant and Dec. She didn't know which one Dec was. I said, 'Do you know which one Ant is?' She said, 'Yes.'

Jimmy Carr

My nan has a picture of the United Kingdom tattooed over her whole body. Some people think it's weird but you can say what you like about my nan, at least you know where you are with her.

Harry Hill

'Get Off The Gas Stove Granny You're Too Old To Ride The Range'

Song title

The word 'good' has many meanings. For example, if a man were to shoot his grandmother at a range of 500 yards, I should call him a good shot, but not necessarily a good man.

G.K. Chesterton

As a child, I went into the study of my grandfather, Winston Churchill. 'Grandpapa,' I said, 'is it true that you are the greatest man in the world?' 'Yes, now bugger off.'

Nicholas Soames

Market research is about as accurate as my grandmother's big toe was in predicting the weather.

Garrison Keillor

I was watching the Superbowl with my 92-year-old grandfather. The team scored a touchdown. They showed the instant replay. He thought they scored another one. I was gonna tell him, but I figured the game he was watching was better.

Steven Wright

We used to terrorize our baby-sitters when I was little – except for my grandfather because he used to read to us from his will.

Jan Ditullio

I'm very proud of my gold pocket watch. My grandfather, on his deathbed, sold me this watch.

Woody Allen

My gently lachrymose grandmother had an extraordinary capacity for reliving the events of the Bible as though they were headline news in the paper.

Peter Ustinov

My grandmother was utterly convinced I'd wind up as the Archbishop of Canterbury. And, to be honest, I've never entirely ruled it out.

Hugh Grant

Helped Grandma with the weekend shopping. She was dead fierce in the grocer's; she watched the scales like a hawk watching a field mouse. Then she pounced and accused the shop assistant of giving her underweight bacon. The shop assistant was dead scared of her and put another slice on.

Sue Townsend, **The Secret Diary of Adrian Mole Aged 13¾**

Oh, Grannie, you shouldn't be carrying all those groceries! Next time, make two trips.

Nathan Lane

Everyone's Favourite Grandmother

QUEEN ELIZABETH, THE QUEEN MOTHER (1900–2002)

The Queen Mother seemed incapable of a bad performance as a national grandmother – warm, smiling, human, understanding, she embodied everything the public could want of its grandmother.

John Pearson

– I'm going to live to be 100.
– Then it will be Charles who'll send you your centenarian telegram.

The Queen Mother and Queen Elizabeth II

I've got to go and see the old folk.

The Queen Mother, 97, spotting a group of pensioners at Cheltenham Racecourse

Is it me or are pensioners getting younger these days?

The Queen Mother, 100, presenting prizes at an old people's garden competition

Horse racing is one of the real sports that's left to us: a bit of danger and excitement, and the horses, which are the best thing in the world.

The Queen Mother

I keep a thermos flask full of champagne. It's one of my little treats.

The Queen Mother

There is all the difference in the world between the patient's meaning of the word 'comfortable' and the surgeon's.

The Queen Mother after she was described as 'comfortable' following an operation

Choppers have changed my life as conclusively as that of Anne Boleyn.

The Queen Mother on helicopters

When one is 18, one has very definite dislikes, but as one grows older, one becomes more tolerant, and finds that nearly everyone is, in some degree, nice.

The Queen Mother

She is a law unto herself and takes no notice of advice.

Aide to the Queen Mother

A glass of wine with lunch? Is that wise? You know you have to reign all afternoon.

The Queen Mother to Queen Elizabeth II

– Who do you think you are?
– Mummy, the Queen.

The Queen Mother and Queen Elizabeth II

For goodness' sake, don't let Mummy have another drink.

Queen Elizabeth II to a pageboy

Don't retouch my wrinkles in the photograph. I would not want it to be thought that I had lived for all these years without having anything to show for it.

The Queen Mother

I love life, that's my secret.

The Queen Mother

Hers was a great old age, but not a cramped one. She remained young at heart, and the young themselves sensed that.

Dr George Carey, Archbishop of Canterbury

She seemed gloriously unstoppable and ever since I was a child I adored her. Her houses were always filled with an atmosphere of fun, laughter and affection.

Prince Charles

Parents and Children

Avenge yourself, live long enough to be a problem
to your children.

Kirk Douglas

All right, since your parents are coming, I did the standard
preparent sweep. Which means if you're looking for your 'neck
massager' it's under the bed.

Jimmy Cox, **Rock Me Baby**

– Homer, are you really going to ignore your father for the rest
of your life?
– Of course not, Marge, just for the rest of his life.

Marge and Homer Simpson, **The Simpsons**

You might notice your ageing parents have both become
abnormally attached to some kind of pet, a dog or a cat that they
got after all the kids left home. They buy it sweaters and birthday
gifts and they have conversations with it that are often longer and
more meaningful than the ones they have with you.

Dave Barry

– Dorothy, why don't we bond?
– Mom, we're from before bonding and quality time.

Dorothy Zbornak and Sophia Petrillo, **The Golden Girls**

Stay another bloody week? Over my dead body! She makes me un-bloody-plug everything at night before we go to bed – but she's got herself a bloody electric blanket on all night.

Jim Royle, **The Royle Family**

– You must miss Prince Andrew, Ma'am, when he's away in the Navy?
– Indeed I do. Especially because he is the only one in the family who knows how to work the video.

Visitor and Queen Elizabeth II

My parents did a really scary thing recently. They bought a caravan. This means that they can pull up in front of my house anytime now and just live there.

Paula Poundstone

My parents live in a retirement community, which is basically a minimum-security prison with a golf course.

Joel Warshaw

Why do so many old people live in those minimum-security prisons? What's with all the security? Are the old people trying to escape, or are people stealing old people?

Jerry Seinfeld

Secrets of Long Life

– To what do you attribute your long life?
– To the fact that I haven't died yet.

Sir Malcolm Sargent

To what do I attribute my longevity? Bad luck mostly.

Billy Wilder

My father died at 102. Whenever I would ask what kept him going, he'd answer, 'I never worry.'

Jerry Stiller

– Happy 103rd Birthday, Mr Zukor. What is the secret of your long life?
– I gave up smoking two years ago.

Adolph Zukor

Good Things About Being the Oldest Person in the World: You make 'The Guinness Book of Records' without doing a damn thing; at your 100th-year high school reunion, you've got the buffet all to yourself; you don't need denture cleaner – you can just call the grandchildren and borrow theirs; you can suck at golf and still shoot your age; you can smoke all you damn well please.

David Letterman

Bad Things About Being the Oldest Person in the World: seems like every time you turn around that damn Halley's Comet is back; shoulder-length ear hair; you get to see your great-great-great-grandchildren marry moon men; all the shoes.

David Letterman

It's a proven fact: gardeners live longer. You are young at any age if you are planning for tomorrow and gardeners are always looking forward, anticipating new shoots.

Mira Nair

You live longer once you realize that any time spent being unhappy is wasted.

Ruth E. Renkl

Women don't live longer. It just seems longer.

Erma Bombeck

Scientists say that women who have children after 40 are more likely to live to be 100, but they don't know why. I think the reason is, they're waiting for the day when their kids move out the house.

Lorrie Moss

– What is your prescription for a healthy long life?
– Never deny yourself anything.

Mr Justice Holmes

Ciggie-loving Marie Ellis was laid to rest yesterday – after living to 105 despite smoking nearly half a million fags. She was cremated clutching a packet of her favourite Benson & Hedges. Staff and residents from the nursing home sent her off with a chorus of 'Smoke Gets In Your Eyes'.

The Sun *newspaper*

Alcohol is good for you. My grandfather proved it irrevocably. He drank two quarts of booze every mature day of his life and lived to the age of 103. I was at the cremation – the fire would not go out.

Dave Astor

I can only assume that it is largely due to the accumulation of toasts to my health over the years that I am still enjoying a fairly satisfactory state of health and have reached such an unexpectedly great age.

The Duke of Edinburgh, 80

My three rules for a long life are regular exercise, hobbies and complete avoidance of midget gems.

Kitty, **Victoria Wood**

I credit my youthfulness at 80 to the fact of a cheerful disposition and contentment in every period of my life with what I was.

Oliver Wendell Holmes

The Oldest Swinger in Town

LOVE AND COURTSHIP

Your place, or back to the sheltered accommodation?

Barry Cryer

Hi, I'm Marv, your grandmother's gentleman-caller, or as you kids would say, her booty call.

Marv, **Rock Me Baby**

'When My Love Comes Back From The Ladies' Room Will I Be Too Old To Care?'

Lewis Grizzard, song title

They say a man is as old as the woman he feels. In that case, I'm 85.

Groucho Marx

Only flirt with women who flirt with you or you can end up looking like those old rich gents in night-clubs, proudly photo-graphed with their arms round bimbos whose interest was clearly in the old geezer's bank balance rather than in his wrinkled and lined person.

George Melly

Hugh Hefner now has 7 girlfriends – one for each day of the week. Someone needs to tell him that those are nurses.

Jay Leno

When we were young, you made me blush,
go hot and cold, and turn to mush.
I still feel all these things, it's true –
but is it menopause, or you?

Susan Anderson

As you get older, the pickings get slimmer, but the people don't.

Carrie Fisher

Gentleman, retired, knocking on a bit. Own teeth and hair. Seeks lady (45 plus) for raw sex.

Lonely hearts ad

Before I turn 67, I would like to have a lot of sex with a man I like. If you want to talk first, Trollope works for me.

Jane Juska, personal ad, **The New York Times Review of Books**

I was introduced to a beautiful young lady as a gentleman in his 90s. Early 90s, I insisted.

George Burns

I don't date women my own age. There aren't any.

Milton Berle

Delighted you came, my dear, and I'd like you to know that you made a happy man feel very old.

Terry-Thomas, the last remake of **Beau Geste**

−You wrote in a story that when you reached the age of 84 you would commit suicide. Why have you not done so?
− Laziness and cowardice prevent me. Besides, I am constantly falling in love.

Jorge Luis Borges

It's never too late to have a fling
For Autumn is just as nice as Spring
And it's never too late to fall in love.

Sandy Wilson

Nothing makes people crosser than being considered too old for love.

Nancy Mitford

I have almost done with harridans, and shall soon become old enough to fall in love with girls of 14.

Jonathan Swift

When one is 20, yes, but at 47, Venus may rise from the sea, and I for one should hardly put on my spectacles to have a look.

William Thackeray

Marriage

When marrying, ask yourself this question: do you believe that you will be able to converse well with this person into your old age? Everything else in marriage is transitory.

Friedrich Nietzsche

It's quite a romantic idea, growing old together. Sitting on park benches, feeding the ducks, leafing gently through *Saga* magazine.

***Dorothy,* Men Behaving Badly**

Walking down the aisle together after they'd just married, Michael Denison turned to his new wife Dulcie Gray and whispered, 'Just think, darling, only 50 years off our golden wedding anniversary!' He died just before they reached their 60th anniversary.

Alan Marks

I want to be married to my wife until we forget each other's names. My wife is the only one who knows what I used to be; and she is starting to lose a little of it too, so we are breaking down in tandem.

Bill Cosby

I've been married so long I'm on my third bottle of Tabasco.

Susan Vass

An archaeologist is the best husband a woman can have; the older she gets, the more interested he is in her.

Agatha Christie

Whatever you may look like, marry a man your own age – as your beauty fades, so will his eyesight.

Phyllis Diller

Carol Channing, 82, star of the hit musical, *Hello, Dolly!,* wrote fondly about her high school sweetheart, Harry Kullijian, in her memoir, *Just Lucky.* Kullijian, 83, read the book, got in touch with Carol, and now they've got married. 'He's exactly the same now as he was when we were 12,' said Ms Channing.

Amy Robinson

We've managed 24 years of marriage – with a lot of broken crockery along the way.

Eileen Atkins

My wife and I have just celebrated our 30th wedding anniversary. If I had killed her the first time I thought about it, I'd be out of prison by now.

Frank Carson

I gave him the best years of my thighs.

Dorothy Zbornak, The Golden Girls

My parents have a very good marriage. They've been together forever. They've passed their silver and gold anniversaries. The next one is rust.

Rita Rudner

My parents stayed together for 40 years but that was out of spite.

Woody Allen

The best way to get a husband to do anything is to suggest that he is too old to do it.

Felicity Parker

When you live with another person for 50 years, all your memories are invested in that person, like a bank account of shared memories. Thus, the past is part of the present as long as the other person lives. It is better than any scrapbook, because you are both living scrapbooks.

Federico Fellini

Love is what you've been through with somebody.

James Thurber

He has a future and I have a past, so we should be all right.

Jennie Churchill, 64, marrying Montagu Porch, 41

Sex

A little old lady in the nursing home holds up her clenched fist and announces, 'Anyone who can guess what I have in my closed hand can have sex with me tonight.' An elderly gentleman calls out, 'An elephant.' 'Close enough,' she replies.

Anon

When the grandmothers of today hear the word 'Chippendales', they don't necessarily think of chairs.

Jean Kerr

I haven't yet reached the stage where I'd agree that liniment oil is a decent replacement for sex.

Stephanie Beacham

It's ill-becoming for an old broad to sing about how bad she wants it. But occasionally we do.

Lena Horne

– There's a man on our lawn.
– Get a net!

Dorothy Zbornak and Blanche Devereaux, **The Golden Girls**

Let's do it! Let's do it! I really want to rant and rave.
Let's go, 'cause I know, just how I want you to behave:
Not bleakly. Not meekly.
Beat me on the bottom with a *Woman's Weekly*.
Let's do it! Let's do it! Let's do it tonight!

Victoria Wood

Pass me my teeth, and I'll bite you.

George Burns

An old broom knows the dirty corners best.

Irish proverb

My mother-in-law was on holiday in Italy with friends in a
villa situated at the end of an unlit, perilous path. A torch was
found to light the way but it had no batteries. 'I know,' said my
mother-in-law's friend, a lady in her early 60s, 'I'll use the ones
out of my vibrator.'

Janice Turner

Of all the faculties, the last to leave us is sexual desire. That means
that long after wearing bifocals and hearing aids, we'll still be
making love. We just won't know with whom.

Jack Paar

If you cannot catch a bird of paradise, better take a wet hen.

Russian proverb

The great thing about sex when you're older is that you don't have to worry about getting pregnant.

Barbra Streisand

I can still enjoy sex at 75. I live at 76, so it's no distance.

Bob Monkhouse

There's a lot of promiscuity about these days, and I'm all for it.

Ben Travers, 94

In the theatre I'm playing, there's a hole in the wall between the ladies' dressing room and mine. I've been meaning to plug it up, but what the hell … let 'em enjoy themselves.

George Burns, 82

On my 85th birthday, I felt like a 20-year-old. But there wasn't one around.

Milton Berle

I prefer young girls. Their stories are shorter.

Thomas McGuane

Now that I'm 78, I do tantric sex because it's very slow. My favourite position is called the plumber. You stay in all day but nobody comes.

John Mortimer

The Gold Watch

RETIREMENT

I'm taking early retirement. I want my share of Social Security before the whole system goes bust.

David Letterman

I have made enough noise in the world already, perhaps too much, and am now getting old, and want retirement.

Napoleon Bonaparte

It is time I stepped aside for a less experienced and less able man.

Scott Elledge

When a man falls into his anecdotage, it is a sign for him to retire from the world.

Benjamin Disraeli

I really think that it's better to retire, in Uncle Earl's terms, when you still have some snap left in your garters.

Russell B. Long

I know how we'll end up in our dotage – my cat, Vienna, stretched across a tennis racket, and me in the local library clinging to the radiators.

Rigsby, **Rising Damp**

Abolish the retirement age. After all, if everyone had to stop working when they reached 65, Winston Churchill would not have been our wartime leader. He was 66 when he became Prime Minister.

Daily Mirror

We spend our lives on the run. We get up by the clock, eat and sleep by the clock, get up again, go to work, and then we retire. And what do they give us? A bloody clock.

Dave Allen

Sometimes it's better to be sacked. I hate the leaving do, and the statutory retirement present, which is always something awful like a gold watch or an engraved wok.

Greg Dyke

Musicians don't retire; they stop when there's no more music in them.

Louis Armstrong

I'll never retire. I won't quit the business until I get run over by a truck, a producer or a critic.

Jack Lemmon

Retire? Did Christ come down from the Cross?

Pope John Paul II

There comes a time when it is too late to retire.

Lord Hailsham

I'm retired. I'm now officially a lower form of life than a Duracell battery. I've been replaced by a box. It's standard procedure apparently for a man my age. The next stage is to stick you inside one.

Victor Meldrew, **One Foot in the Grave**

After I retired, I fished a lot, dove a lot, boated a lot – and made Johnny Walker Red about a quarter of a million dollars richer.

Dennis Diaz

What do gardeners do when they retire?

Bob Monkhouse

What shall I do now I'm retired? I thought I might grow a beard … give me something to do.

Victor Meldrew, **One Foot in the Grave**

I make the coffee, Barbara makes the beds, and we're right back to square one where we got married when we were 20 years old.

George Bush, former US President

My husband has just retired. I married him for better or for worse, but not for lunch.

Hazel Weiss

Gotta Lotta Livin' To Do

There will come a time when you believe everything is finished.
That will be the beginning.

Louis L'Amour

I want to tell people approaching and perhaps fearing age that
it is a time of discovery. If they say, 'Of what?' I can only answer,
'We must find out for ourselves, otherwise it won't be a
discovery.'

Florida Scott-Maxwell

Look, I don't want to wax philosophic, but I will say that if you're
alive you've got to flap your arms and legs, you've got to jump
around a lot, for life is the very opposite of death, and therefore
you must at the very least think noisy and colourfully, or you're
not alive.

Mel Brooks

Let's not go out and get denture cream. Let's go to the nude
beach and let our wrinkled selves hang out! We'll sit on the
boardwalk and watch the old men rearrange themselves when
they come out of the water.

Sophia Petrillo, The Golden Girls

Do not grow old, no matter how long you live. Never cease to stand like curious children before the Great Mystery into which we were born.

Albert Einstein

I am more alive than most people. I am an electric eel in a pond of goldfish.

Edith Sitwell

When you're young, you don't know, but you don't know you don't know, so you take some chances. In your 20s and 30s you don't know, and you know you don't know, and that tends to freeze you; less risk taking. In your 40s you know, but you don't know you know, so you may still be a little tentative. But then, as you pass 50, if you've been paying attention, you know, and you know you know. Time for some fun.

George Carlin

Life is a great big canvas, and you should throw all the paint on it you can.

Danny Kaye

Write, paint, sculpt, learn the piano, take up dancing, whether it's the tango or line-dancing, start a college course, fall in love all over again – the possibilities are limitless for you to achieve your private ambitions.

Joan Collins

Singing, fishing, meeting my close and dear friends, looking at pictures and nature, shocking a few people who deserve shocking, taking my pills, writing a book and swigging Irish whiskey. These are my ways of fending off the old gent with the scythe waiting patiently to harvest me.

George Melly

I use my increased leisure time to look at paintings wherever there is a gallery, to enjoy opera and drama at a theatre, to visit country houses.

Denis Healey

Life isn't measured by how many breaths we take, but by the moments that take our breath away.

Chinese saying

Sometimes I would rather have someone take away years of my life than take away a moment.

Pearl Bailey

We should do something that will make your heart dance once a day. If you can't do that because you're too depressed, then do something that will make somebody else's heart dance.

Yoko Ono

There were days last winter when I danced for sheer joy out in my frost-bound garden in spite of my years and children. But I did it behind a bush, having a due regard for the decencies.
Elizabeth von Arnim

I get up before anyone else in my household, not because sleep has deserted me in my advancing years, but because an intense eagerness to live draws me from my bed.
Maurice Goudeket

Most people say that as you get old, you have to give up things. I think you get old because you give up things.
Theodore Green

Develop interest in life as you see it: in people, things, literature, music – the world is so rich, simply throbbing with treasures, beautiful souls and interesting people. Forget yourself.
Henry Miller

I wouldn't mind turning into vermilion goldfish.
Henri Matisse, 80

Enjoying sex, loving fashion, having fun, decorating our homes, going on lavish holidays – the list is endless. Onward!
Joan Collins

It is a mistake to regard age as a downhill grade towards dissolution. The reverse is true. As one grows older, one climbs with surprising strides.

George Sand

You have to take time out to be old. I'm still full of piss and vinegar.

Paul Newman

If old people were to mobilize en masse they would constitute a formidable fighting force, as anyone who has ever had the temerity to try to board a bus ahead of a little old lady with an umbrella well knows.

Vera Forrester

I work every day and I want to die shouting *mierda*.

Joan Miró

I can't actually see myself putting make-up on my face at the age of 60. But I can see myself going on a camel train to Samarkand.

Glenda Jackson

At past 50, I solemnly and painfully learned to ride the bicycle.

Henry Adams

You should make a point of trying every experience once, excepting incest and folk-dancing.

Anon

I hope I have a young outlook. Since I have an old everything else, this is my one chance of having a bit of youth as a part of me.

Richard Armour

In a boat I lost 20 or 30 years straight away.

Helen Tew, 89, trans-Atlantic sailor

The only time I've ever been rendered speechless with fury was when some daft television presenter opened a programme aimed at senior travellers by asking what sort of holidays were 'suitable' for them. 'Any and all they really want to take,' is the short answer.

Elisabeth de Stroumillo

Cruising: if you thought you didn't like people on land …

Carol Leifer

I don't want to get to the end of my life and find that I lived just the length of it. I want to have lived the width of it as well.

Diane Ackerman

Signs You're on a Bad Cruise: the brochure boasts the ship was the subject of a 60 Minutes exposé; as you board, a personal injury lawyer hands you his business card; no matter what you order from the bar, it tastes of salt; every time you see the crew, they're wearing life-jackets; the vessel's name is the S.S. *Scurvy*.
David Letterman

I'd like to learn to ski but I'm 44 and I'm worried about my knees. They creak a lot and I'm afraid they might start an avalanche.
Jonathan Ross

I now realize that the small hills you see on ski-slopes are formed around the bodies of 47-year-olds who tried to learn snowboarding.
Dave Barry

There isn't anybody who doesn't like to see an old man make a comeback. Jimmy Connors seemed like a jerk to me until he was 40. After that, I rooted for him all the time. How could you not?
T. Boone Pickens

Golfers grow old and try to shoot their age. It must be a terrific feeling when someone asks your age and you can say, 'Par.'
The Pittsburgh Post

The older you get, the stronger the wind gets – and it's always in your face.
Jack Nicklaus

A Quiet Life

A QUIET LIFE

I once wanted to save the world. Now I just want to leave the room with some dignity.

Lotus Weinstock

As I grow old, I find myself less and less inclined to take the stairs two at a time.

Bernard Baruch

I turn 70 this year and all of a sudden the horizon that once seemed far away looms right there in front of you. You feel an irresistible urge to slow down, to take your foot off the accelerator, touch it to the brake – gently, but surely – and start negotiating yourself out of the fast lane.

Bill Moyers, former White House Press Secretary

I am 72 years of age, at which period there comes over one a shameful love of ease and repose, common to dogs, horses, cler-gymen and even to Edinburgh reviewers. Then an idea comes across me that I am entitled to 5 or 6 years of quiet before I die.

Rev. Sydney Smith

Even under a harsh God, one is entitled to serenity in old age.

Albert Outler

What is wrong with settling down with a good book into a rocking chair by the fireside, wearing a comfy pair of slippers if that is what makes you happy?

Eloise Pagett

I love this time of day. When I'm sitting here in my own little home, with my own wonderful little hubby, and we talk about issues of the day and discuss world affairs and generally just snuggle.

Mavis Wilton, **Coronation Street**

I used to have a sign over my computer that read, 'Old Dogs Can Learn New Tricks', but lately I sometimes ask myself how many more tricks I want to learn. Wouldn't it be easier to be outdated?

Ram Dass

If old age in the shape of waning strength says to me often, 'Thou shalt not!', so do my years smile upon me and say to me, 'Thou needst not!'

Mary Vorse

It's only natural that a person becomes quieter as they grow older. They've got more to keep quiet about.

Samuel Butler

One's first step to wisdom is to question everything – and one's last is to come to terms with everything.

Georg Christoph Lichtenberg

Growing older, I have lost the need to be political, which means, in this country, the need to be left. I am driven into grudging toleration of the Conservative Party because it is the party of non-politics, of resistance to politics.

Kingsley Amis

When one has reached 81, one likes to sit back and let the world turn by itself, without trying to push it.

Sean O'Casey

The members seated in the pavilion at the Test Match declined to join in the mexican wave. Well, when you get to a certain age, every time you just get out of your chair, it's a bit of an adventure.

Henry Blofeld

Old men are dangerous; it doesn't matter to them what is going to happen to the world.

George Bernard Shaw

Rest is not idleness, and to lie sometimes on the grass on a summer day listening to the murmur of water, or watching the clouds float across the sky, is hardly a waste of time.

John Lubbock

Silver Surfers

TECHNOLOGY

– Mother, are you still on the computer?
–Yes, dear. Sometimes you get into a porn loop and just can't get out.

Edina and her mother, **Absolutely Fabulous**

Here I sit, a modern Werther Original. Not telling dusty fairy stories to my 4-year-old and feeding him teeth-rotting toffees but teaching him how to work my computer so that one day soon he can teach me things.

Peter Preston

A great way to meet the opposite sex when you're older is on the Internet, a good reason to learn to use a computer. The Internet is 70 per cent men, so the odds are definitely in a woman's favour for finding a guy.

Joan Rivers

My nan said, 'What do you mean when you say the computer went down on you?'

Joseph Longthorne

Age and Youth

I am getting older in a country where a major religion is the Church of Acne.

Bill Cosby

When I was young there was no respect for the young, and now that I am old there is no respect for the old. I missed out coming and going.

J.B. Priestley

I'm quite happy about growing older. Who wants to be young? Being 18 is like visiting Russia. You're glad you've had the experience but you'd never want to repeat it.

Barbara Cartland

Youth is something very new: 20 years ago no one mentioned it.

Coco Chanel, 1971

We are happier in many ways when we are old than when we are young. The young sow wild oats, the old grow sage.

Winston Churchill

Young people know the rules. Old people know the exceptions.

Oliver Wendell Holmes

I've got things in my refrigerator older than you.
Lee Trevino to Tiger Woods

When I see a young girl I view her with the same pity that she views me with.
Lilli Palmer

Old people have one advantage compared with young ones. They have been young themselves, and young people haven't been old.
Lord Longford

There's one thing I have over any 21-year-old: a proud history of accumulated neuroses.
Ray Romano

Never have I enjoyed youth so thoroughly as I have in my old age.
George Santayana

Young men wish for love, money, and health. One day, they'll say health, money, and love.
Paul Géraldy

Age is not an accomplishment, and youth is not a sin.
Robert Heinlen

The Good Old Days?

In my old age I find no pleasure save in the memories which I have of the past.

Giacomo Casanova

We have all got our 'good old days' tucked away inside our hearts and we return to them in dreams like cats to favourite armchairs.

Brian Carter

I have liked remembering almost as much as I have liked living.

William Maxwell

Reread all the letters you've kept over the years – the wonderful thing is, you won't have to answer them.

Thora Hird

When we recall the past, we usually find that it is the simplest things – not the great occasions – that in retrospect give off the greatest glory of happiness.

Bob Hope

In July, when I bury my nose in a hazel bush, I feel 15 years old again. It's lovely! It smells of love!

Camille Corot

One of the oddest things in life, I think, is the things one remembers.
Agatha Christie

In memory, everything seems to happen to music.
Tennessee Williams

– Do you remember the minuet?
– Dahling, I can't even remember the men I slept with!
Tallulah Bankhead

– During the …
– If you say during the war, I'll pour this cup of tea over your head!
– I wasn't going to say during the war! Bloody little know-all!
– Alright then. Sorry.
– That's alright. During the 1939–1945 conflict with Germany…
Del Boy Trotter and Uncle Albert, **Only Fools and Horses**

I never saw a banana till I was 14. I was immediately sick after eating it and haven't touched one since.
Enid Bray

I remember when the wireless was something useful. In my day you could warm your hands on the wireless and listen to Terry Wogan. Nowadays all you can do is listen to Wogan.
Paula Brett

In my day, we never got woken up by a teasmade. We were knocked up every morning by a man with a 6-foot pole … And we weren't having hysterectomies every 2 minutes either, like the girls these days. If something went wrong down below, you kept your gob shut and turned up the wireless.

Old Bag, **Victoria Wood**

In my day, there were things that were done, and things that were not done, and there was even a way of doing things that were not done.

Peter Ustinov

In my day, a juvenile delinquent was a kid who owed tuppence on an overdue library book.

Max Bygraves

My generation thought fast food was something you ate during Lent, a Big Mac was an oversized raincoat and 'crumpet' was something you had for tea. 'Sheltered accommodation' was a place where you waited for a bus, 'time-sharing' meant togetherness and you kept 'coke' in the coal house.

Joan Collins

Always have old memories and young hopes.

Arsene Houssaye

Thank You for Being a Friend

FRIENDSHIP

As life goes on, don't you find that all you need is about two real friends, a regular supply of books, and a Peke?

P. G. Wodehouse

We need old friends to help us grow old and new friends to help us stay young.

Letty Cottin Pogrebin

One consolation of ageing is realizing that while you have been growing old your friends haven't been standing still in the matter either.

Clare Boothe Luce

The mere process of growing old together will make our slightest acquaintances seem like bosom-friends.

Logan Pearsall Smith

I don't have a warm personal enemy left. They've all died off. I miss them terribly because they helped define me.

Clare Boothe Luce

When you're 50 you start thinking about things you haven't thought about before. I used to think getting old was about vanity – but actually it's about losing people you love. Getting wrinkles is trivial.

Joyce Carol Oates

If I had any decency, I'd be dead. Most of my friends are.

Dorothy Parker

The loss of friends is a tax on age!

Ninon de Lenclos

All my friends are dead. They're all in heaven now and they're all up there mingling with one another. By now, they are starting to wonder if I might have gone to the other place.

Teresa Platt

Going, Going, Gone!

DEATH

Like everyone else who makes the mistake of getting older,
I begin each day with coffee and obituaries.

Bill Cosby

I get up each morning and dust off my wits,
Pick up the paper and read the obits.
If my name isn't there I know I'm not dead;
I have a good breakfast and go back to bed.

Anon

Why did I not do more in my life, I ask myself, as I read the
obituaries of the people who have crammed their lives with
'doing' while I have wasted great chunks of mine dreaming?

Mary Wesley

My old mam read the obituary column every day but she could
never understand how people always die in alphabetical order.

Frank Carson

I have never killed a man, but I have read many obituaries with
great pleasure.

Clarence Darrow

When I get in a taxi, the first thing they say is, 'Hello Eric,
I thought you were dead.'

Eric Sykes

I have been dead for two years, but I don't choose to have it
known.

Lord Chesterfield

There are so many ways of dying, it is astonishing that any of us
choose old age.

Beryl Bainbridge

There are worse things to die of than old age.

Clive James

How young can you die of old age?

Steven Wright

Hope I die before I get old.

Pete Townshend

Statistics tell us that Audrey Hepburn died young. What no
statistics can show us is that she would have died young at
any age.

Peter Ustinov

I want to die young at an advanced age.

Max Lerner

Jesus died too soon. If he had lived to my age he would have repudiated his doctrine.

Friedrich Nietzsche, 48

I don't mind dying. Trouble is, you feel so bloody stiff the next day.

George Axelrod

It seems like the only two times they pronounce you anything in life is when they pronounce you 'man and wife' or 'dead on arrival'.

Dennis Miller

– When we die, certain things keep growing – your fingernails, the hair on your head, the hair on your chest…
– Not the hair on my chest!
– My dear, you give up hope too easily.

Lawrence Olivier and Edith Evans

For three days after death, hair and fingernails continue to grow but phone calls taper off.

Johnny Carson

Better take my photograph now, dear – I'm 80, I might die at lunch.

Lady Diana Cooper to a magazine photographer

At a formal dinner party, the person nearest death should always be seated closest to the bathroom.

George Carlin

I am ready to meet my Maker. Whether my Maker is ready for the ordeal of meeting me is another matter.

Winston Churchill, on his 75th birthday

My family has a propensity – it must be in our genes – for dropping dead. Here one minute, gone the next. Neat. I pray that I have inherited this gene.

Mary Wesley

– How would you like to die?
– At the end of a sentence.

Interviewer and Peter Ustinov

My dream is to die in a tub of ice cream, with Mel Gibson.

Joan Rivers

Let me die eating ortolans to the sound of soft music.

Benjamin Disraeli

Mottoes to Live By

If you wake up in the morning, then you're ahead for the day.

Mace Neufield

You can't turn back the clock. But you can wind it up again.

Bonnie Prudden

You're never too old to become younger.

Mae West

It's never too late to be what you might have been.

George Eliot

I think, therefore I still am.

Elliott Priest

If you rest, you rust.

Helen Hayes

You're only old once!

Dr Seuss

Live well, learn plenty, laugh often, love much.

Ralph Waldo Emerson

If not now, when?

Hillel the Elder

Live your life as though your hair was on fire!

Anon

Learning and sex until rigor mortis!

Maggie Kuhn

Never pass a bathroom.

Duke of Edinburgh

Don't take life so seriously. It's not permanent.

Kathy Holder

Exercise daily. Eat wisely. Die anyway.

Anon

May you live all the days of your life.

Jonathan Swift

Live your life and forget your age.

Norman Vincent Peale

Index

Picture Credits

The publishers would like to thank the following sources for their kind permission to reproduce the pictures in this book:

Alamy Images: /ImageState: 146

Corbis Images: /ABM/zefa: 50; /Caterina Bernardi/zefa: 18; /Fabio Cardoso/zefa: 30; / William Coupon: 26; /Susanne Dittrich/zefa: 110; /Nick Dolding/Zefa: 58; /Nick Dolding/ zefa: 22; /Jean Michel Foujols/Zefa: 102; /Jean Michel Foujols/zefa: 86; /Patrik Giardino: 118; /Mark Hamilton/zefa: 126; /John Henley: 142; /Jutta Klee: 42; /C. Lyttle/zefa: 66; /Mauritius: 34; /Darren Modricker: 6; /Jens Nieth/zefa: 54; /Anna Peisl/Zefa: 10; /M. Petosa/Photex/zefa: 134; /Darius Ramazani/zefa: 46, 70, 154, /Gary Salter/zefa: 38; /Sygma: 98

Getty Images: /Archive Holdings Inc: 94

Photolibrary.com: /Images.com: 78; /Workbook Inc: 62

SuperStock: /Francisco Cruz: 106; /Tony Garcia: 138; /Mauritius: 114; /age fotostock: 14, 82, 90, 122, 150

Every effort has been made to acknowledge correctly and contact the source and/or copyright holder of each picture and Carlton Books Limited apologises for any unintentional errors or omissions which will be corrected in future editions of this book.